PSYCHOLOGICAL FIRST AID

AND

THE GOOD SAMARITAN

Other Titles by Dr. Larry Wonderling

Non-Fiction

SEDUCTIVE ILLUSIONS, *How to Resist the Lure of Society's Smoke and Mirrors*

SAN FRANCISCO TENDERLOIN,
True Stories of Heroes, Demons, Angel, Outcasts, and a Psychotherapist, Expanded Second Edition

MINDING YOUR MATTER, *A Breakthrough Health and Fitness Model Without Formal Diets and Exercises*

Fiction

THE ULTIMATE EVIL, *A San Francisco Mystery Novel*

DEAD MANNEQUINS, *A Mystery Novel,*
A Sequel to The Ultimate Evil

PSYCHOLOGICAL FIRST AID

AND THE GOOD SAMARITAN

By Larry Wonderling, Ph.D.

Cape Foundation Publications
Dewey, Arizona
Email: capfound@aol.com

CAPE FOUNDATION PUBLICATIONS
Dewey, Arizona
Email: capfound@aol.com
Carol Eversole, Editor
Norman Cyr, Cover Design

ISBN: 0-9659415-9-0
ISBN 13: 978-0-9659415-9-4

TABLE OF CONTENTS

PART VI
The Mental Health Paradox

DEDICATION

I often think of those innocent 20 Sandy Hook school children and adult victims, some of whom might have been spared had the killer received earlier treatments for obvious mental problems.

I also dedicate this book to the American Red Cross whose First Aid Manuals have saved countless lives.

PROLOGUE

Victims in crisis come in all sizes, shapes, ages, pain thresholds, and I.Q.'s—just like Good Samaritans. Their suffering may be primarily medical, psychological, or both with an equal range of intensity. Ironically, however, offering first aid to a physically injured victim is generally more straightforward than attempting to initially help someone experiencing emotional pain or mental torment.

Assisting a psychologically injured victim, who just lost his child or witnessed a murder, is infinitely more difficult than helping a victim with a broken arm. Red Cross First Aid rules are much more easily understood than psychological ones. The physically injured have strikingly similar anatomies, while the psychologically injured can be markedly different in their reactions to stress. Mental and emotional responses to an internal or external crisis situation vary with each individual, depending on the person's unique background, personality, defensive resilience, support systems, genetic predisposition, and even their gender. While one person can witness the gory mutilation and death of a loved one with mild psychological or physiological effects, another person experiencing a similar trauma may succumb to physical shock, resulting in their premature death if not treated.

In 1972 I worked as a consultant psychologist for the Peace Corps in Afghanistan. During a training group's first free weekend in over a month, three of the trainee married couples experienced a potentially life-threatening, traumatic incident. The couples, all in their

twenties and thirties, ventured beyond the training center in Kabul to explore the countryside. Picnicking in a lush meadow below the magnificent fourteen thousand foot Salang Pass, they waved at a passing squad of Afghan soldiers who were apparently on their way to Kabul. Within twenty minutes, the three husbands were thoroughly and painfully bound and gagged. Lying on their sides, they watched in agonizing desperation as their wives, about four feet away, were stripped naked and repeatedly raped by ten teenage Afghans. The ordeal lasted for less than an hour, and as abruptly as it began, the soldiers vanished, leaving the women naked and husbands bound and gagged.

This indelible memory may be the perfect lead-in to this book by exploring an incident with "potentially" traumatic psychological consequences. Some of you may be frowning in wonderment. "What do you mean potentially? Anyone who experiences such an event would be devastated." Well, not everyone.

Back to the three naked women and their hog-tied husbands: Between medical exams, each couple was interviewed by me within an hour of their return to the training camp. During the interview with the first couple, the wife sobbed uncontrollably while the husband railed through gnashing teeth against Afghanistan and those "scrawny rag heads."

The second couple was more philosophical. Both were concerned about being sent home before being sworn in as volunteers, they felt they should have never waved at the soldiers, and that they had a lot to learn before effectively serving in a third world country. Although tearful, the wife had recovered since their return and her major concern was getting a venereal disease.

The third couple was surprisingly cavalier about the entire episode. The wife grinningly opened the interview with assurances that she'd coped with tougher situations in New York, along with the unblinking comment that most of the "kids" were nervous and couldn't "get it up." Her husband was mild-mannered, politely responsive to questions, and wore a fixed smile.

Ironically, this couple separated during the last month of training, which had nothing to do with the incident. The wife went home and her estranged husband successfully completed his two year service in the Afghan city of Kandahar.

The first couple was air-evacuated home within a week of the situation, and the second couple was later considered outstanding volunteers while stationed in Afghanistan's Mazar-i Sharif. As a footnote, two weeks after the incident was reported to Afghan officials, the military commander summarily ordered the arrest and execution of ten soldiers despite an absence of identification by any of the couples.

Ψ Ψ Ψ

Ever since my Korean military service and such Peace Corps experiences, I have considered the possibility of a mental health first aid manual. These events in my life have underscored the marked individual differences in responding to the same external stressors. People simply don't react the same when exposed to disastrous situations, no matter how psychologically traumatic.

You have probably known a WWII, Korean, Viet Nam, or more recent Iraq or Afghanistan veteran who has suffered from PTSD, psychotic episodes, or eventually committed suicide as a probable result of earlier combat experiences. You have no doubt also known countless veterans with virtually the same combat experiences who quickly readapted to civilian life with no significant mental or emotional sequel.

Other professional experiences in ghettos and prison jobs surrounded me with alcoholics, drug substance abusers, and a wide variety of outcasts, misfits, and consummate victims. Such vast individual differences in psychological responses to external situations again underscored one of the basic reasons for this book. *People's responses to traumatic or distasteful events throughout their lives will somehow affect how they react to any future traumatic events they encounter.* This complex assortment of rational and irrational behaviors is difficult to understand or predict, even by the well-trained professional. Consequently, trying to assess and offer first aid treatment to the mentally disturbed is far more confusing than assisting a physically injured person. Also, different from most physical injuries, psychological wounds don't necessarily occur immediately after a trauma. They may gradually emerge in days, weeks, or even years. Those long forgotten events may create insidious behavioral peculiarities that personally affect their family and friends. These aberrant behaviors manifest themselves in a variety of ways that might represent a personal menace to others. Identifying such problem behaviors and their effects on significant others may be described as "second aid," which is another critical reason for this book.

As we age, it becomes increasingly apparent that, al- though we may generally look and act alike, human behavior is markedly complex, while individual differences range from the "Mother Teresa saintly" to the "Jack the Ripper evil." Our kaleidoscope of individual behaviors also comes from an endless variety of influences, including individual genomes, birth place, family environment, stability, friends, and all sorts of other positive and negative external experiences: including addictions, drug substance abuse, disease, overwhelming traumas, long term subtle abuses, etc., etc.

The cost of the psychological effect of these negative behaviors on our society is astronomical in considering death and injuries from violent behaviors, imprisonment, mental institutionalization, etc. Hence another reason for this book, which is divided into six parts to more clearly cover the separate yet interrelated topics.

Part I is about becoming a Good Samaritan. Part II is the psychophysiology of bizarre behavior. Part III defines mental disorders. Part IV defines the various dementias. Part V is second aid for those you know. Part VI is the mental health paradox.

Such vast individual differences in psychological response to external or internal stressors underscore the primary reason for this book. Assessing and administering first aid treatment to the emotionally or psychologically traumatized is infinitely different from initially helping the physically injured. As I said earlier, different from most physical injuries, psychological wounds resulting in strange or menacing behaviors can emerge months, even years, after the initial trauma. This may further complicate an intervention strategy, which is another reason for this book.

Having acquainted you with the vital need for such a book, here's a promise: Once you read this book, your understanding of psychologically disturbed people and your readiness to help them will have markedly increased your confidence and understanding in deciding when to directly help and when to find help for those in need.

INTRODUCTION

American Red Cross First Aid books have been a part of home libraries since the green covered first edition appeared over a hundred years ago. Those invaluable manuals have taught the average person, with negligible medical knowledge, how to perform lifesaving procedures, from restarting the heart and resuscitation, to stopping arterial bleeding. As valuable to the first aider, such information has provided them with a powerful sense of self-confidence in initially treating physical injuries.

The actual lives saved by simple first aid procedures over the past one hundred Red Cross years of First Aid books are no doubt astronomical; especially in considering how such vital first aid information has gradually spread through countries throughout the world. It's also noteworthy that each revised edition, now into the third millennium, has updated medical findings while further simplifying those initial lifesaving first aid procedures.

Recognizing the miraculous lifesaving power of these easily understood books, I distributed them to many Peace Corps volunteers while providing a basic first aid course to those assigned to remote areas in third world countries. The effect was astonishing. With limited medical clinics available in many Peace Corps service areas, local residents began to rely on Peace Corp volunteers to render first and second aid care for their physical injuries. Some volunteers also gave basic first aid courses to interested villagers.

Back then, however, there were no first aid manuals available that included initially aiding emotionally traumatized persons. I had also learned early in my own professional practice, that the complexities of individual differences in emotional response to similar situations probably discouraged such a manual. The average high school graduate today is aware that the most effective first aid treatment for all non-breathing victims is Cardiopulmonary Resuscitation (CPR.). Crisis victims of abuse or other emotional traumas, however, may present by externalizing their grief with anger or rage, while other crisis victims may internalize with sobbing, guilt, and suicide thoughts.

Today, the only emergency information still absent from first aid books seems to be the immediate treatment of bizarre mental and emotional behaviors associated with traumatic psychological events. As a clinical psychologist, it has become increasingly apparent to me that psychological injuries are as pervasive as medical ones in any disaster, yet less understood, and with few clear cut treatment procedures consensually validated as effective in emergency situations. In other words, there didn't seem to be any evidence-based initial help for the emotionally traumatized that the average bystander could offer. Nevertheless, I began to recognize that filling the psychological gap in first aid manuals would be a worthwhile, albeit monumental task.

That's when I concluded: the glaring absence of studies related to psychological first aid, such a psychological first aid treatment manual was definitely needed. Then I could at least start with existing intervention strategies—to be expanded with further research.

Obviously, assessing strange behavior is typically more complex than trying to figure out if bleeding is in need of direct pressure or if the absence of breathing or a pulse requires CPR. The Good Samaritan is also less likely to offer assistance to a disoriented person acting crazy, drunk, on other street drugs, or possibly violent.

Even most police, with basic first aid knowledge and some domestic violence training, don't quite know how to deal with weird behaviors. Although law enforcement officers patrolling the streets are certainly more likely to encounter emergency situations that invariably include unusual behaviors, they are usually more focused on crime prevention, enforcing laws, controlling potentially life threatening behaviors, evaluating the scene for possible criminal activity, and providing other support functions. These include crowd control, protection of EMT's and other professionals performing their essential services.

Nonetheless, law enforcers aren't on patrol just to arrest criminals. They're expected to serve the public by responding to such reports as disturbing the peace, public domestic squabbles, or some scary crazy person wandering a neighborhood. Law enforcement or other public service agencies typically may have basic first aid training; however, fundamental psychological interventions in helping the emotionally disturbed remain sketchy at best.

The extent of law enforcement psychological training tends to vary considerably within and between states. Some counties, for example, have victim advocacy training for volunteers to assist law enforcement during crisis situations. Others have ongoing human relations training, while other law enforcement agencies are more focused on arresting criminals than assessing behaviors.

The noteworthy differences in agency's law enforcement training strategies, professional biases, and local attitudes are further suggested by the variable handling of bizarre behaving individuals who may present a danger to themselves or others. As examples, newspapers frequently report police initial responses, such as the subduing of a club-carrying male suspect by police officers using a stun gun. The incident occurred in Nevada. Then there was the Arizona police shooting death of an enraged 5'3" mother with her two children present. She was reportedly brandishing a small knife while surrounded by several male police officers. Also in Arizona a lone police officer talked a 6'2" machete-wielding suicidal male into dropping his weapon and going to an emergency room. In California a naked black man was chased by two police officers who momentarily caught and subdued him. After putting on his shorts, he ran again and when grabbed, he fought both officers with his fists until one officer shot the unarmed man to death.

Such documented cases of varying police strategies when faced with a strange behaving, potentially dangerous person underscore both the need for basic mental health training and accepting the reasonable reluctance of any untrained potential Good Samaritan from approaching a visibly distraught or traumatized person. It also points up the marked personal differences in responding to potentially threatening situations, regardless of training. Even well-trained officers, like combat troops, may respond unpredictably to an emotionally confusing, personally threatening situation.

In researching the mental health training of police officers, I distributed a survey to a wide range of police departments, with questions about training in dealing with bizarre behaviors. The responses were not too surprising in that many department heads indicated comprehensive mental health training of their patrol officers; while a significant number of the "beat" cops' personal comments suggested they didn't feel sufficiently trained to deal with the mentally disturbed.

A letter from a prominent San Francisco police department head in 2010 clearly stated that police officers were receiving solid mental health intervention training for 40 hours. In 2011, however, an article in the San Francisco Chronicle reported the San Francisco Police Commission was reviewing the way the mentally disturbed suspects were being treated by police officers. The article indicated that "In the past year or so officers have killed at least three disturbed men and wounded another. Mental health providers suggest these shootings could have been avoided or de-escalated if the officers had been better training." One of the commission's conclusions was that experienced mental health professionals should be providing services too often attempted by poorly trained police officers. Since then the San Francisco Police Commission has unanimously approved training up to a quarter of the city's police officers as a crisis intervention team modeled after a Memphis Tennessee program that has dramatically reduced dangerous mental illness situations.

Another encouraging advancement in law enforcement human relations has recently been occurring in Wichita, Kansas. Their police department has developed a brand new unit to deal with the homeless problem in their city. Rather than repeatedly arresting the homeless for "intoxication or urinating in public" the homeless outreach team assists them in finding housing, health care, jobs, and mental health counseling including drug and alcohol rehabilitation programs. This social work oriented unit has been operating since February 2013, and during the first five months, so many homeless have been place in housing facilities and programs, there are waiting lists.

All of these findings clearly underscore the noteworthy differences in police department's procedures, training, and scope of their concerns throughout the nation. It also underscores the many reasons why even compassionate bystanders may tend to run from behaviors they don't understand! To them it may be the mysterious unknown. It could be dangerous, and besides, they're not qualified to help. Others, however, will disregard such risks in order to help someone in distress, despite their vague assessment of the situation. Both such extremes could use some training.

Such concerns were probably similar in physical injury situations before those vital first aid books and courses that offered a confidence-building "cookbook" of life saving instructions. Even today, despite, or perhaps because of our civilized social savvy and scientific sophistication in the 21st century, the average citizen shies away from trying to cope with, let alone help, strangers exhibiting weird behaviors. As suggested above, there are also others with more courage than prudence that may take charge and end up exacerbating the situation.

Although I've long acknowledged a need for some sort of emotional crisis supplement to traditional first aid manuals, it took me an additional twenty years before I was ready to seriously tackle such a project. It finally became apparent that *comprehensive simplicity* would be essential. Otherwise the average high school grad might not bother to read it. I also decided that, in dividing the book into six separate parts, it would need to include easily understood information related to basic psychology, types of bizarre symptoms, dealing with abusive behaviors by family or friends, and the mental health dilemma in the United States.

This book, however, is definitely not a course in psychology requiring academic prerequisites; and it has avoided psychotherapeutically flavored theoretical constructs related to the treatment of abnormal behaviors. Nor is it a disaster training manual. There are many national and international organizations that have fine manuals and training courses for the "first responder" volunteers to assist victims of flood, fires, earthquakes, and manmade disasters such as war's inevitable "collateral damage." The titles of these disaster manuals are indexed in the Appendix under References.

Psychological First Aid will, however, give you a basic understanding of individual differences in human behavior, a straight forward set of guidelines when encountering a mentally or emotionally troubled person, evaluating bizarre symptoms, and most important, knowing when to personally help friends, relatives, or strangers, and when to run for help!

Finally Part VI discusses how the incredible advances in technology and pharmacology during the last one hundred years has failed to effectively acquaint today's average person with a basic understanding of bizarre behavior requiring professional assistance. Moreover, how "medicalizing" emotionally troubled persons, primarily with drugs, has interfered with a practical understanding of a wide variety of strange behaviors.

The erroneous assumption is that the average person hasn't the skill to assist an emotionally troubled person with medical interventions. *Psychological First Aid* is just that, initially helping a strange-behaving person until the arrival of professional help that ironically may or may not require pharmaceutical interventions. The ordinary person with no medical, pharmaceutical, or psychological backgrounds will always remain desperately needed as "a Good Samaritan."

PART I

Preparation

The Webster's New World College Dictionary defines the Good Samaritan with biblical implications as *a person who pities and helps another or others unselfishly*. While such selfless aid to others in the past has clearly required plenty of compassion, the more complex psychological first aid in the third millennium may involve many other human attributes as well.

In today's crowded, socially stressful urban societies, people aren't accustomed to spontaneously helping others, especially those exhibiting strange, disturbing behaviors. In addition to compassion, approaching a stranger exhibiting weird behaviors may also demand selflessness and courage, as well as a good dose of common sense.

Helping the physically injured in the pioneer days, long before Red Cross books, must have immediately triggered reflex compassion and empathy. Survival concerns then were probably a major preoccupation in such a rugged, sparsely populated country where helping each other survive another day was routine!

In today's hectic, industrialized society with no shortage of people, including medical professionals, too many of us assume someone else, more qualified, will assist the physically or emotionally injured stranger. In some beltway communities, however, many people are a bit wary when even approached by a stranger asking for the time of day. It has become a *none of my business* response to unexpected or unsettling behaviors by strangers.

It may surprise you that I actually agree with a silent majority who leaves first aid interventions, psychological or physical, to the appropriate professional provided they're available. That's just plain common sense. Trying to stop bleeding when you're prone to faint at the sight of blood, approaching an emotionally troubled person when afraid of so-called "crazies," or jumping into a lake to help a drowning child when you can't swim are usually self-defeating behaviors that defy common sense and jeopardize the emergency. However, here's an often repeated caveat throughout this book. An appropriate decision by some bystanders may understandably be to do nothing other than "get help."

True, courage is frequently a prominent quality in those who try to aid others. Yet, once aware of our limitations, common sense may be a more vital quality in retreating from traumatic situations we discover too late that we simply can't handle. Consequently, Part I provides readers with a self-assessment venue to assist in deciding just how prepared they are as modern day Good Samaritans.

CHAPTER 1

A Bystander's Dilemma

As suggested above, not everyone is capable of administering first aid regardless of the victim's symptoms and the actual situation. When our pioneer great grandparents encountered a physically or mentally injured settler, they had few choices, knowing professional help was unavailable. In the third millennium we have plenty of choices, even when we're first on a traumatic scene.

Since we're always with ourselves, all we need to immediately know is our personal, physical, and mental limitations before courageously plunging into a situation that ultimately we may be unable to effectively handle. Paradoxically the busier and more populated a community, the less likely we are to spontaneously help strangers. Perhaps such complex communities have become reluctant to initiate helping others, because they are suspicious of others' motives, they're unprepared for the unpredictable, they are just too dehumanized to really care, or they assume someone else will help. There's a phrase for this last possibility. It's called *the bystander effect*.

A fundamental premise in this chapter is the certainty that no matter how cautious, careful, or self-protective we are in any environment, we simply can't avoid the possibility of confronting a traumatic, bizarre, or disturbing situation. It happens, and the question is, what do we do when the unexpected occurs?

This is why Chapter 1 is primarily devoted to helping our readers grasp their own strengths and weaknesses as a potential Good

Samaritan before critically exploring the specific basic training requirements of a Psychological First Aider.

Although compassion, common sense, and courage (the three C's) seem to be essential catalysts that inwardly encourage someone to assist a total stranger, common sense is no doubt the most reflective of the three. It's needed as a thoughtful hesitation in making an initial decision to spontaneously approach or prudently retreat from a disagreeable situation.

Many outcomes of our toughest decisions in life, however, are unpredictable even to the cautious, prudent decision maker. That's until the final moment when there's just an instant to reflexively change our minds.

Perhaps the real paradox is that we all tend to look and act somewhat alike until most routine life situations are interrupted by an ominous, threateningly disruptive occurrence. Then differences emerge that reveal to all, our thinly veiled uniqueness as individuals. It's a revelation that may remind us that some of our strengths and weaknesses still haven't been challenged by an unexpected event. That's when our "persona" yields to basic, primordial instincts.

Since we may not know our visceral selves as clearly as we think, the following questionnaire might provide a few additional personal insights to help you initially explore your Good Samaritan readiness. Simply number a blank sheet of paper from one to twenty. Then score each item with either a 1 meaning no agreement, to 10, meaning total agreement. Any number in between, such as a 5, indicates more or less some agreement.

Remember this questionnaire isn't a psychological test with a comprehensive, standardized score; it's simply a self-assessment tool to facilitate a closer look at your unique self under unusual conditions.

Questionnaire

1 I'm a real people-watcher whenever I'm out in public.
2 I like to get involved in whatever's going on around me.
3 I would openly report anyone abusing an animal.
4 I'm hardly ever upset by unexpected street behaviors.
5 If I thought someone was trying to physically hurt someone, I would try to stop them or call for help.
6 I've experienced helping others in emergency situations.
7 I've rarely backed away from a heated argument.
8 I have deep compassion for the underdog.
9 I have a few friends with such close loyalties I'd defend them no matter what.
10 I generally feel fairly comfortable when a nearby stranger is acting weird or emotional.
11 I'm typically frank in giving feedback to acquaintances who offend me.
12 Loud noises don't particularly bother me.
13 If I encountered someone with an obvious injury, I wouldn't hesitate to help.
14 I'm not uneasy when approached by an adult male stranger.
15 I usually help those unfortunates who can't help themselves.
16 In helping an emotionally traumatized person, it doesn't matter how big and strong you are.
17 Even when alone I'll verbally defend my principles when violated by a group.
18 I don't mind witnessing unusual situations that I don't quite understand.
19 If I were to hear someone nearby screaming for help, I would quickly try to find the person as the first step in assessing the situation.

20 I completed the American Red Cross Basic First Aid course.

Now that you've completed your twenty item self-analysis, add up your scores. Since there's a maximum of ten points each, a total score of over two hundred points represents a basic elementary school math problem. If, however, you accurately score a total of two hundred, you may be the old west gun-slinger type, always ready to courageously and passionately rescue anyone in distress. This can be an admirable yet risky lifestyle.

Such a high score is rare and includes Medal of Honor winners and people like Wesley Autry, the New York subway guy, who saw a man fall onto the rails of an approaching train. After asking some nearby ladies to watch his two girls, he leaped off the subway platform, and when unable to pull the injured man to safety, he covered the victim with his own body as the train ran over them. He is one of my most revered heroes, perhaps because I doubt that I would have had the courage to risk my life under such circumstances. In retrospect, he didn't seem to have sufficient time to evaluate the risk involved, especially in protecting the victim with his own body while not knowing if he had enough clearance.

To some, he must have been suicidal, arguing that a prudent bystander, aware of personal limitations would have declined the heroism. Then there are others who believe courage and compassion simply preempted common sense. My point is that in such potentially perilous situations, even the most prudent Good Samaritan really doesn't know the outcome until it's over! As a footnote, Mr. Autry, who was over 50, African-American, with two children, didn't hesitate to risk his life for a young Caucasian male.

Of course, most efforts to help someone aren't that dangerous, yet each event demands that the bystander make the same lonely, very personal, critical decision—to help or not. So, as you examine your questionnaire responses you might keep in mind two profound behavioral adages. 1. You are what you do, not what you say you are. 2. The best prediction of future behavior is your past behaviors.

Then again ask yourself: Have you ever been the first at the scene of an injured person? What did you do to help? What couldn't you do? Have you encountered other traumatic situations? Again, what did you do, and what did you learn about yourself?

If you've never had such first on the traumatic scene experiences, have there been other events in your life that underscore your strengths and frailties? Maybe a friend or relative is beginning to act a bit peculiar. You suspect drug abuse, possible physical abuse of his wife. He could become dangerous. What do you do or what did you do?

Having completed the questionnaire and explored its additional implications, you may wonder if there are any specific personality characteristics for a Good Samaritan. I personally don't think so; however, some general guidelines may be helpful:

- Age doesn't matter. There's the well-documented case of the four-year-old dialing 911 for his critically ill mother; and the seven-year-old boy who pulled his unconscious younger brother from their swimming pool, administered CPR that he learned in school, while telling his hysterical mother to call 911.

- Effective common sense responses to life's crises are linked to neither gender nor academic degrees. In fact, a memorable comprehensive longitudinal study years ago indicated that the major characteristics of the most revered clinical psychologist, teacher, or counselor ranked highest in empathy, naturalness, good listener/observer, and nonjudgmental. Academic achievements, age, and gender were ranked low in importance. Don't forget the highly variable responses by those professional police officers to bizarrely behaving persons.

- Making correct decisions in life is another irrelevant requirement for the Good Samaritan. In fact, recognizing that we're fallible humans who are forever capable of wrong decisions may be an essential prerequisite to Good Samaritan status. As grandma used to say, "Nobody's perfect, not even you."

- Having no physical or intellectual limitations that might interfere with helping a stranger, is also a dash of nonsense. Look within yourself carefully enough and you'll find a variety of reasons for avoiding uncomfortable situations. Yet, ultimately knowing and accepting one's limitations is indispensible when faced with those critical life situations.

- Having just turned the corner, you see a disheveled man walk into the street, do a slow-motion rolling fall on the asphalt, and rock back and forth in a sitting position while moaning that nothing else matters. Quickly assessing the situation and your own limitations, you call 911, because you have no idea what has prompted his weird behavior or what he's up to. Did you make the appropriate decision? I really don't know. I believe in that situation, alone with a stranger exhibiting peculiar, possibly menacing behaviors that for me personally, a 911 call to professionals was certainly the most prudent decision. Obtaining immediate help to stop any oncoming traffic might also be advisable.

- There are also Good Samaritan laws in virtually every state to provide legal protection for bystanders who offer emergency care to a physically or emotionally troubled individual. These laws offer legal immunity to anyone who provides emergency treatment "in a reasonable and prudent manner while expecting nothing in return." There are, however, exceptions to immunity from prosecution and laws that are covered in the next chapter.

Readers may have figured out by now that this book discourages heroism. The qualified Good Samaritan's most sensible and helpful decision when faced with a perplexing bizarre situation may be to give help by quickly getting help. You may have personally noticed that police officers, fire fighters, emergency medical technicians, and other professionals are seldom heroes. They don't typically engage in hand-to-hand combat with a deranged, knife-wielding person. They don't race into a burning building about to collapse, nor do they apply medical aid to some victim if exposed to sniper gun fire. Despite or because of professional training, their decisions are usually based on well-practiced procedures that are likely to emphasize their own safety first and discourage heroism while serving others.

Most such professionals patrolling our cities are nice folks, just like us. The main difference being their job that trains them exceptionally well to protect and care for others as they protect and care for themselves.

A nationally reported mine death in March 2011 exemplifies the very human and professional dilemma regarding this approach vs. retreat from a victim whose life may depend on you. A worker in Nevada falls 200 feet down an abandoned mine shaft. A video reveals this poor man has severe injuries, yet he's still breathing as he lay trapped by debris at the bottom of this century old, unstable mine. One rescuer's initial attempt to descend to the victim resulted in a large falling rock splitting his hard hat, with further crumbling rocks and debris hurtling down the shaft. As a consequence, the rescue was suspended and rescuers remained above as the 28-year-old father of five gradually died. Both rescuers and family later reported "shock and disbelief" when instructed to discontinue the rescue attempt. All those involved said it was the most frustrating experience they had ever encountered.

Nationally, the controversy was clear, as readers of the death in newspapers throughout the country insisted "no one should be abandoned in such a situation." Securely ensconced in one's home, such courageous arguments—like Monday morning quarterbacking—may be well-meaning, but calling off the rescue was apparently the only rational decision to protect others.

Then there's the U.S. Airways Flight 1549 near disaster. Although passengers on the flight understandably praised Captain

"Sully" Sullenberger as a quintessential hero, I consider him the perfect example of a well-trained professional. He followed emergency procedures within the parameters of his limited choices; which resulted in the saving of everyone's life, including his own. Had he been alone on the aircraft, he would have undoubtedly followed the same procedures as an experienced, competent professional, not a hero.

Perhaps that's what this Chapter 1 on a potential Good Samaritan's behavior is really about: spontaneously helping others within the limits of your experience and personal training; while avoiding behaviors that may endanger your welfare or the victim you're trying to help.

Even before this book offers any clearly delineated procedures, when you, a bystander, encounter a bizarre behaving stranger, there's a clarion call you'll keep hearing throughout this book: *Call 911 and if no cell phone, ask someone else to call immediately to get professional help ASAP.*

Finally, keeping in mind that Good Samaritans may not be well-trained, salaried professionals, the following summarizes the initial reflections of a Good Samaritan: Typically he or she is a bystander without the forewarning of a weird behaving stranger that may need immediate help. The bystander may never encounter such a stranger or may bump into a desperately disturbed person within the hour. As an unprepared person, you have a few seconds to decide whether to help or ignore. Perhaps an expansion of Hippocrates' prudent suggestion to physicians to "do no harm," should include Good Samaritans doing no harm to themselves as well.

If you're prepared to at least make certain 911 is called for professional assistance, you, as a bystander, for that moment have entered Good Samaritan territory. Rather than reason "it's none of my business" you're trying to help. So, welcome. You may be a Good Samaritan already!

CHAPTER 2

Good Samaritan Prerequisites

It's worth repeating that Good Samaritans aren't defined by the amount or quality of their help, but by their selfless, willingness to try to help, rather than walking by a possible victim. Such bystanders are the ones who never really intended to confront a disturbing situation. They never planned to be a Good Samaritan.

This chapter moves beyond the bystander's initial experience as a potential Good Samaritan. It's about readers who intend to assist the troubled, if or when necessary. It's for those who want to increase their potential as an affective Good Samaritan. As a consequence, it may be of value to start with legal issues related to helping traumatized strangers.

Are Good Samaritans vulnerable to law suits? They certainly are, at least in the United States. Are Good Samaritans legally liable if the assistance exacerbates the victim's problems? That depends. These are two independent legal issues. For the first, we're virtually all "sueable," yet most everyone that tries to help a stranger isn't ultimately "liable." Unfortunately, we seem to live in a lawsuit-driven country where the well-intending Good Samaritan is sued by a troubled man whose arm was injured during the struggle when he was physically stopped from committing suicide off the Golden Gate Bridge.

In those states I researched, however, the court records suggest that lawsuits against bystanders trying to help an endangered stranger are extremely rare. Those plaintiffs that actually sue such bystanders also rarely win against a Good Samaritan who exhibited good intentions, with no evidence of intentionally further harming the trauma victim, performing intrusive treatment without the appropriate medical training, or willfully contributing to the added injury of a victim because of abusive behavior.

Although I haven't read liability standards in all 50 states, nor am I an attorney, I doubt that anyone meeting all the Good Samaritan requirements in this book would be found legally liable after trying to help a traumatized stranger.

The Transition from Bystander to Good Samaritan

So, other than having a cursory understanding of the possible legal consequences, how do you prepare to give immediate aid to a stranger who is doing something you never anticipated? How do you prepare yourself for an emergency incident that may never happen? These are some of the more obvious questions to help determine just how and when you actually become a Good Samaritan.

You may have figured out by now there's obviously no strict criteria, no applause, no fanfare with a roll of the drums, and no certificate emblazoned in gold leaf. Spontaneously and unexpectedly you're suddenly a Good Samaritan; not because you think you are, it's because you acted like a Good Samaritan. Remember, "We are what we do" not what we think we are.

So, in lieu of an actual event, try roll-playing the following *virtual* event of an anonymous bystander called "Joe." This may help you grasp some idea of how the average person might react when unexpectedly confronted with a bizarre situation.

Having a morning stroll down a street in your neighborhood, Joe (aka you) is suddenly faced with a bizarre behaving stranger, and notices blood flowing through the saturated right sleeve of his sweater.

Think about your initial response to this unexpected situation. Remember there are no right or wrong answers in how each individual spontaneously tries to voluntarily help a troubled stranger. Pardon the cliché but it "all depends on a variety of things." Even if this stranger gratefully survives following Joe's personal efforts, other decisions might have been just as effective or more effective, or as you'll learn later in this book, some victims of your first aid help may try to sue you.

In any event, whatever you do or don't do, there's one action that is always justified. If you, the bystander, personally decide approaching this stranger is too scary, an immediate 911 call by you, Joe, or anyone else, qualifies as a Good Samaritan. Knowing your limitations, you helped in the only way you could while not ignoring his apparent need for help. Anytime you feel unable to help, yet find some safe way to assist—welcome. You're no doubt also a good neighbor and a good person! As for what an experienced, knowledgeable first aider would actually do to help the victim in this chapter, will be explained in detail in Chapters 3 and 4.

Now, back to the stranger acting disturbingly weird with what may be a bleeding, oozing right arm. Congratulations, if you, in your roll-play, agreed with the 911 call. No matter what you do or don't do after your call, you at least have a pretty good idea that the police and EMT's will eventually arrive to professionally assist this troubled person. You hope it's soon, yet you just don't know how long it will take before they arrive. You also don't know if the arriving police have been appropriately trained to deal with bizarrely behaving strangers. In any event, their training is irrelevant to your decision to call 911, your first and perhaps most sensible decision since you're convinced you're not really qualified to do much more. In fact, if you hang around much longer, you may be late for work. Anyway, there are other people forming who are probably more qualified to help than you—the bystander effect.

As you read the above situational scenario, including the first on-the-scene bystander, Joe, with no experience, confidence, or courage to deal with an unpredictable, possibly dangerous situation, you may have had vicarious twinges of empathic agreement, sympathy, or even contempt for his actions or inactions. Yet, regardless of a bystander's age, gender, education, interpersonal skills, altruism, and readiness to help others, just how one will cope with the unpredictable threat is ah… unpredictable. So, if you were critical of this particular bystander, he deserves some slack. As I said earlier, his actions are certainly worthy of congratulations and here's why. Despite his initial "none of my business" reluctance to do anything other than rationalize a hurried exit to work, he dialed 911.

If I seem to be repeating myself, well, I am. One of my themes throughout this book is the critical gap between doing nothing or something. So long as people in our society avoid at least calling 911 when faced with a strange, frightening situation, many serious mental or physical injuries will continue to accrue and remain undocumented.

No bystander, regardless of trauma background would have any clear idea if the bizarrely behaving stranger was suicidal, homicidal, an accident or assault victim, in life threatening shock, panic attack, drug overdose, drunk schizophrenic, or exhibiting some sort of idiopathic seizure disorder, etc., etc. Most health care professionals will no doubt agree that virtually any inexperienced bystander will be understandably puzzled, frightened, and initially debating what to do; while walking or running by is probably the first option.

This initial decision is extremely important for both victim and our society. Most of us live in an electronic age of civilized people scurrying about in some crowded city that invites suspicions and a mistrust of strangers, especially weird ones. It's not surprising that the "none of my business" syndrome is so prevalent in modern society. For too many, our society has also become increasingly dehumanized, resulting in an attitude of indifference to the plight of others.

Newspapers offer countless accounts of this syndrome and its tragic results. As examples, several years ago a young woman in New York City screamed for help as she was brutally beaten and raped. This occurred during the early evening in a well-populated neighborhood. No one tried to intervene by even shouting at the assailant or calling the police.

In the outskirts of San Bernardino, California at rush hour, a man later identified as a serial killer of a dozen women, chased a screaming passenger down the side of the heavily trafficked highway. The victim had escaped from his slow moving car, and as she banged on other car windows begging for help, the assailant caught her and began dragging her back to his vehicle. Still no one in the slow traffic tried to intervene with a shout or cell phone call. Fortunately for her, a motorcycle cop on his way back to the station noticed the attack and arrested the man who surrendered without resisting.

In San Francisco, a distraught man leaped to his death off the Golden Gate Bridge as a crowd of onlookers quietly watched.

Such incidents are frequently unreported while underscoring how the initial sight of someone acting strangely or even terrified too often triggers fear of involvement or an overwhelming sense of personal threat. Such a reaction can shock the bystander into an understandable avoidance reaction; which is another reason for this book: *To encourage those ready to run, "none of my business" bystanders to become a Good Samaritan by simply dialing 911 or its more primitive substitute, "a shout for help."*

CHAPTER 3

Situational Assessment

In the last chapter, Joe was instinctively ready to walk by a conspicuously distasteful situation, and as a knee-jerk reaction, most of us would agree it's an understandable consideration. Without the luxury of a few reflective moments and a little rehearsal time, it may be difficult to judge just how you might respond to some "crazy" in apparent need of help. Then there's your common sense alternative thought to run for it.

It's also worth remembering that even well-trained first responders, professional health care workers, or police officers frequently experience that fear reaction when confronted with a potentially disruptive person. However, after overcoming that involuntary flight reflex, they let their training kick in with some fundamental principles that also apply to a potential Good Samaritan bystander:

1. Observe! In virtually any profession that initially deals with strangers in emergencies or just in need of assistance, *observation* of the strange, irrational behavior and the surroundings are vital in essentially all situations. All doctors, including veterinarians, dentists, physicians, chiropractors, and clinical psychologists certainly agree that careful observation is vital to an affective practice.

    You may have noticed that humans are voraciously visual, despite their other four prominent senses. We constantly make decisions based on what we see, from the casual to the critical. Unless our vision is somehow impaired, we ironically take our ability to see for granted, to the extent that we're often unaware of our limited visual attention to our surroundings. It's amazing how much we unconsciously omit from our visual field even in our own neighborhood. I missed noticing that quaint looking red front door of the old house across the street from my house, after a two year residence. When grandpa would trip over a curb, grandma would give the proverbial caution, "look where you're going."

It's equally amazing how much we can absorb from changing situations when presented with anticipated visual cues. Buy a new car and you suddenly begin noticing your model car parked everywhere. That's an especially important principle when unexpectedly approaching a bizarrely acting stranger. It's the perfect time to practice expanding your observations; which include listening, "smelling," and possibly some touching.

2. During this first encounter, keep a six to ten foot distance as you observe this possible victim. Estimate the person's approximate age, e.g., child, teenager, adult, or senior. What's the person wearing, general grooming, facial expressions, holding any objects, any blood or other signs of wounds, posturing, movements, any mumbles or audible words, and if eyes are open. Who is the victim looking at? Are there odors, like alcohol, feces, etc? Expectations have plenty to do with the scope of our visual attention, and you'll be pleasantly surprised by the amount and variety of information available to your conscious memory by just following the above suggestions once you see a troubling situation.

3. What's your specific location, how many other bystanders, street traffic, businesses, etc? These are also vital bits and

pieces of visual information as you quickly assess the overall situation. Arriving professionals are grateful for such observations.

4. In evaluating the potential victim's behavior and appearance, you will probably have some more reflective opinions regarding the need for medical assistance, mobility, level of consciousness, and violence potential. Al-though all of those possibilities will be discussed in Part II, I'll emphasize again that, at this juncture in your observations, if you've paused for a few minutes, assessed the situation, concluded professional opinions are warranted, made sure 911 was called, and awaited their arrival while concluding you're unable to do anything else, congratulations, you are then a Good Samaritan!

CHAPTER 4

Approach Decision

Once you have assessed the situation and await the professionals, be aware their arrival time may vary from five minutes to a half hour—or more. As Joe, (you) your initial assessment revealed one obvious injury, indicated by the blood flowing from the victim's right arm. Since you have had no first aid training, you don't know how to stop the persistent bleeding. Otherwise the victim seems well enough to await medical attention. So, what should you do while waiting? If you're still reluctant to physically approach the victim, you should talk to other bystanders, especially the one who may have called 911 for you. One of them might have sufficient first aid knowledge to help this troubled victim. As a Good Samaritan, reminding others of the still bleeding arm and your lack of first aid training is certainly appropriate, while letting them make their own personal decisions about their readiness to actually help.

If, however, you (aka Joe) had a basic first aid course and depending on your observation of the victim's behavior, you might suggest to him to apply *direct pressure* to the bleeding and assure him that you'll stay with him until the professionals arrive.

Loss of blood from excessive bleeding can be life-threatening, within minutes. Consequently, if you have such basic first aid knowledge, ask the victim, while you maintain a distance, if you could help him to stop the bleeding. That's provided, after observing him for a few minutes, the victim is too weak or passive to be a threat to others.

While awaiting the arrival of professionals, you may also ask other bystanders for help if they know basic first aid. You certainly don't have to be hesitant about discussing a weird victim with other bystanders, which may result in bystanders offering assistance. It's an interesting phenomenon that, in a crisis, when many possibly qualified bystanders are doing nothing but watching, it takes just one person's comments to prompt them to help. Nationally, such a human catalyst as Martin Luther King and the Republic of South Africa's Nelson Mandella clearly hastened the laws against racial discrimination in the U.S.A. and South Africa. Too frequently, without a person who assumes the role as leader, the oppressive status quo will continue. So don't ever be hesitant about asking other bystanders for help or assistance as a potential Good Samaritan.

PART II

Basic Behavioral Psychophysiology

As one of my personal biases, I strongly encourage anyone interested in helping other strangers in any sort of distress to take the basic American Red Cross First Aid course which will ultimately provide you with a greater sense of confidence in your readiness to assist others, as well as having invaluable lifesaving skills. In fact, psychological first aid isn't exclusively first aid for the psyche; it invariably includes decisions related to the physical appearance and actions of any stranger with their unique individual differences.

Consequently, completion of a first aid course will inwardly encourage you to more comfortably look beyond the peculiar behavior to the stranger's physical characteristics. You may even notice some physical anomaly suggesting an injury. Arriving professionals are grateful for such information.

Hippocrates, the father of modern medicine, also had it right when he said prophetically over 400 years ago, "It's far better to treat the patient with a disease than the disease of the patient."

CHAPTER 5

The Mental Status Examination (MSE)

This is an essential part of a procedure well known to most medical and mental health professionals; and despite its Mental Status title, it's a uniform, detailed way of initially developing a behavioral portrait of a person. Its basics are also well worthwhile to the Good Samaritan.

- Basically, these initial observations by a lay person begin with the first thing we tend to notice when we encounter a bizarre behaving stranger. As a prelude to the Mental Status Examination (MSE) that first observation represents the virtual snapshot of a human who silently records as female or male, skinny or fat, well-groomed or disheveled, big or small, attractive or grotesque, while also observing their ethnic characteristics, and unusual facial features, including tattoos, piercings, scares, etc. that may be of added significance.

- Then, almost instantaneously, the visual appearance becomes alive with movement that quickly translates into mannerisms; and before you know it, this emoting human is unwittingly defined by your perceptual field as predator, prey, victim, pitiful, disgusting, performing, threatening, etc.

- Your opinion of this stranger doesn't matter much unless there's something in your interpretation that triggers an uneasiness about his/her possible urgent need for medical, psychiatric, or police attention!

- As I suggested earlier, this behavioral portrait may provide sufficient information for that 911 call vs. a ho-hum "walk by" or an oh-oh "run by." Just remember that each of these three responses is one of countless decisions you make daily; however, since this one may be a life saver, be a Good Samaritan and dial 911 if you lingered long enough to have some doubts about the normalcy of this stranger's physical and mental condition.

- Again, observing a stranger's unusual behavior in an effort to evaluate the person's physical and mental condition is the initial step of any professional patient assessment, and your 911 call simply suggests a more thorough observation may be warranted.

- Your basic MSE further includes a thorough observation of bizarre, weird, strange, crazy, or out of control actions. At this point you obviously don't need any psychodiagnostic training to know when someone's observable behavior is sufficiently unusual to seem frightening, threatening, or plain disgusting. You just need to focus for a while on what the stranger is doing.

- Having gathered some cues from your observations that the professionals might call symptoms, you may have a few hints about what this stranger's up to. Does he/she resemble a bum, hippie, Goth, or wild street hustler who likes upsetting or entertaining normal bystanders? Or maybe piercing eye contact or no eye contact may suggest rage or indifference to surrounds. Is posture intense with clinched fists, erect, or limp, sluggish, and defenseless, with arms loosely hanging, hunched torso, etc?

- Activity level will range from excessive manic movements with possible flailing arms, etc., fidgety, restless and agitated, to the increasingly subdued, drowsy, to the comatose.

- Attitudes and mood are frequently conveyed with facial expressions in addition to movements. That range from calm and pleasant, dull and phlegmatic, to angry, hostile, belligerent, irascible, and sullen.
- Although your abbreviated MSE observations of this weird-acting stranger have given you an awareness of the person's appearance, activities and mood, his/her verbalization may at least finalize your possible 911 decision. You're obviously not prepared or even interested in exploring articulation, cognition, even fluency. All you need to know is if speech is coherent enough to understand, or if his speech further supports weird, "nutty" behavior. As I suggested in Chapter 4, if the stranger hasn't spoken, simply keep your distance, look directly at the stranger and ask in a calm, pleasant, concerned way if he/she needs any help. Whatever the response or no response, you will most likely know what to do; and as usual, if you still have doubts regarding the person's welfare, call 911!
- Your mini-MSE is obviously your decision-making menu, resulting in your 911 call and possible interaction with the victim or continued observations until the professionals arrive. As I've mentioned before, it's also important to note that most medical technicians and police will be interested in who called 911 and information regarding the victim's observed behavior. Needless to say, Good Samaritans, as defined above, play an indispensible role in assisting the mentally or physically injured. Ironically, these Good Samaritans are unpaid, untrained, and too frequently unacknowledged first responders before the arrival of the well-organized professional first responders. These bystanders, that are now Good Samaritans, have my profound admiration!
- As a reader, you may be wondering just when you *don't* call 911. That decision may be tougher than you think. Our

rule of thumb is, when in doubt about the strange-acting person's well-being or possible danger to others, always call 911. If, however, you realize the person is just performing for attention or money, with such clues as a nearby container with money, a casual outstretched hand, walking by is certainly appropriate. This decision may never be a certainty, and if there are even hints this person may need some sort of professional help, leave the final decision to the 911 professionals.

Finally, the odor of alcohol may suggest that he's "just another drunk." I believe, however, if the associated behavior is indicative of anger, offensively bizarre, or distraught, calling 911 is vital. Just remember, drunks can be violent to others or suicidal; which at least warrants observation by professionals.

CHAPTER 6

Psychological Shock

This behavioral disturbance, also known as traumatic shock, is frequently encountered following an auto accident or other injuries. Consequently it tends to be easily identified by most bystanders. These psychological shocks occur to victims of all ages following disasters such as floods, fires, earthquakes, violent episodes, and, of course, the ravages of war. Victims of these various disasters are generally assisted by well-trained volunteers known as "first responders." They are usually contacted by such agencies as the Red Cross, etc. Immediately following a national disaster, however, sometimes there's no evidence of a traumatic situation other than a visibly terrified or numb, traumatized victim. Yet the symptoms are fairly obvious to the average bystander. These symptoms include many of the PTSD symptoms in Chapter 8. As explained earlier, even though physiological shock (physical injuries) is more likely to kill you, psychological shock affects may persist for years.

Those immediate symptoms of psychological shock, with their physiological components, include dizziness, rapid shallow breathing, etc. along with crying, sobbing, vomiting, etc. All of those symptoms are also very similar to victims of Panic Disorder, Acute Distress Disorder, and related anxiety disorders. With an anxiety, component symptoms may clearly reflect sobs, tension, irritability, restlessness, faulty concentration, shortness of breath, and a sense of feeling on edge, and in need of help. Many traumatic victims will verbally acknowledge their need for help

Following your observations and a 911 call, consoling and reassuring with warm expressions of understanding are vital. Such a Good Samaritan approach is certainly similar to helping those with cognitive disorders as in dementias.

If the victim has a visible injury, simple questions regarding the injury, with appropriate help, depending on the Good Samaritan's skill, may be necessary. If nothing else, helping the victim obtain a warm resting position with legs elevated is generally advisable. Again, any physical first aid help will depend on the Good Samaritan's first aid knowledge, assessment of any life threatening injuries, and readiness to ask other available bystanders for possible assistance depending on their first aid knowledge.

CHAPTER 7

Basic Drug Abuse Symptoms

Biochemically we humans resemble a huge test tube loaded with certain chemicals that keep us alive and well. Adding additional chemicals, e.g., other pharmaceutical or street drugs can cause predictable psychological and/or physiological changes from euphoria to death. Another medical finding, however, is our individual, unpredictable differences in how each human will react to the same drug. As a consequence, many psychotropic drugs that produce their desired prescribed affect usually cause a few unique symptoms, so it's essential to keep in mind in reviewing drug symptoms that there's considerable overlap between drug abuse syndromes.

Alcohol

As a post-prohibition booze-oriented society, these symptoms are probably the most obvious to spot in any situation, ranging from the thoroughly uninhibited giggling goofy; the stumbling, laughing, happy-go-lucky; the word slurring loud and staggering; the "what are you lookin' at" belligerent; the flailing, uncoordinated, obnoxious aggressor; the near stupor, disoriented, "falling down" drunk; etc. Although heavy drinkers are apt to seriously hurt themselves more than others, drunks become increasingly dangerous to others when operating a motor vehicle, which underscores their characteristic faulty visual/motor coordination, reckless bravado, and resultant poor judgment. Needless to say, another obvious symptom of acute alcohol abuse is the smell of alcohol, along with abnormal behaviors.

Following our observation of the weird behaving intoxicant, it's decision time. As usual for the potential Good Samaritan, your decision is based on high probability visual hints that the drunken stranger may need medical attention, as evidenced by bloody injuries, breathing problems, apparent unconsciousness, inability to care for himself, or a possible danger to himself or others, any abusive or bizarre shouting, walking or staggering into the streets, etc. Once you have called 911 you've done a service to the victim and the community, and since most drunks rarely respond to sober reasoning, just keep observing the victim until the professionals arrive.

During your wait, you can keep the person out of further harm's way (falling into oncoming traffic, etc.) or give basic first aid to severe injuries, within the limits of your knowledge and abilities. Don't ever forget that most domestic violence and traffic crashes are caused by intoxication, more popularly known as "drunks." So, if you notice an obvious drunk entering his car or a potentially violent shouting argument between two possible drunks, don't hesitate to call 911.

Cocaine

In recent decades cocaine hydrochloride, a powder, has been an addictive drug, especially popular with celebrities; while non-powder crack cocaine is a solid, prepared with water and baking soda, cheaper to market, and easily smoked in vapor form with a faster euphoric affect than the powder form. Crack is obviously more popular with lower income, non-celebrities, while crack symptoms are also much more intense.

Any cocaine use can result in a wide variety of symptoms, including paranoid, homicidal, and suicidal thoughts, as well as hallucinatory and delusional psychotic-type symptoms with anger and aggressive outbursts.

Opioids

Many of you have probably experienced mild to moderate opioid intoxication, even though you've never purchased or were given a street narcotic such as heroin. Many of the most effective pain killers, following an injury or surgery, are derivatives of opioids and close cousins to heroin.

Senior citizens probably know more about opioids than their third millennium children. Pain killers such as morphine and other opium derivatives are generally the drugs of choice, especially following serious operations. Heroin, a morphine cousin, is also both a medically prescribed pain killer and widely used street drug. Interestingly, these are highly addictive Schedule I drugs, and they still remain a popular street drug. Legal prescription drugs today, however, are beginning to challenge traditional illegal drugs because of easy access, cost, and demand.

In fact, in your body are narcotics called indigenous opioid peptides such as endorphins, while popular opioid pharmacy drugs include Darvon, Percocet, and Oxycodone. These are all derivatives of street drugs, including methadone and benzodiazepine. The general symptoms include pupillary dilation or constriction, drowsiness or coma, slurred speech, impairment of memory, etc. Violence is rare.

Other Legally Prescribed Drugs

These medications are typically prescribed for relief from pain, depression, anxiety, and psychotic symptoms. As a bystander, there is certainly no need to identify the pharmaceutical names of all these prescription drugs. It is, however, worthwhile to be conversant with the similar symptoms caused by overuse of some of these drugs for recreation. Such drugs also result in accidental coma or even suicide. They include amphetamines, methadone, acetaminophen, codeine, and a wide variety of opioids like phencyclidine (PCP). Prescribed neuroleptics (Phenothiazine and chlorpromazine). Psychotropic drugs (Thorazine), anxiolytics (barbiturates).

The following are many of the similar symptoms of the above drugs when overused:

- Pupil dilation.
- Oscillating eyes.
- Seizures and coma (uncontrollable shaking, unconsciousness).
- Impaired judgment (behaving stupidly or childishly).
- Poor coordination (stumbling, staggering).
- Confusion (can't respond appropriately to simple questions).
- Vomiting (suggesting toxic effects of drugs, including alcohol).
- Psychomotor agitation or retardation (stomping around to gain coordination, or sluggish movements).

You may encounter many of these unusual symptoms while walking down any street in virtually any city in the United States. Although none of these symptoms are indicative of high violence potential, it's important to remember that a physiologically or psychologically disturbed person with the above similar symptoms are all capable of unpredictable aggressive outbursts of a dangerous nature if somehow provoked. Consequently, always initially view a strange-behaving person as capable of angry responses to quick motions by well-meaning bystanders. That's why Chapters 4 and 5 focused on carefully observing a stranger's behavior before approaching.

From this point on, during your transition from bystander to Good Samaritan, it's important to remain aware that even those strangers exhibiting non-threatening behaviors could react violently if somehow provoked by a well-meaning person like you. So the best approach is an outwardly warm, calm, gentle behavior that is not likely to aggravate the stranger's stress level or fears. The message you offer should be, "I'm a warm, non-threatening Good Samaritan who is worried that you may need help and I'm simply here to assist you without ordering you to do anything." Just offer a soft, warm smile, introduce yourself and ask how you can help. Use clear, concrete, easily understood questions. Be respectful as you submissively try to learn how you can assist. If the troubled person doesn't respond, or resists help despite his weird behavior, don't argue or try to force the person to do anything. Just remain concerned and let the person assert some control as you listen at a distance. Also remain clear with short replies, while keeping a non-threatening distance.

As you observe the strange-behaving victim, if you notice symptoms of pain or injuries, tell him or her that professional help is on the way. Also avoid such clichés as everything is fine—when it isn't, or that you know how he feels. Be humbly patient and reassuring while waiting for the EMT's.

Young drug users that experiment with all sorts of substances have recently pursued the use of every day bath salts, which is a stimulant similar to amphetamines and a wide variety of herbal mixtures called "spice" which contain synthetic cannabinoids designed to mimic THC (marijuana). These spices are typically licensed as herbal therapy, while bath salts are marketed as plant food or insect repellant.

Bath salt symptoms include increased alertness and energy with debilitating side effects such as insomnia, nausea, panic attacks, extreme paranoia, and both visual and auditory hallucinations. Spice symptoms are similar to marijuana, yet side effects are more pronounced and dangerous, e.g. hallucinations, seizures, agitation, vomiting, and headaches. Both of these relatively new substances are life-threatening and have not been thoroughly tested. These readily available substances are included to underscore the availability of potentially dangerous drugs for young people.

Drug pushers and plenty of teenagers are constantly searching for cheap chemical fixes. Our youth tend to initially explore their parents' medicine cabinets, followed by combining an assortment of harmless chemicals, plants, and herbs for trial and error use, along with their school "grape vines" and basic high school chemistry as possible drug resources.

The older, more experienced drug users have also developed convincing scams to obtain physician prescriptions for a wide variety of drugs that provide a recreational "high" when used to excess. For our third millennium generation the internet is also a rich source of information relevant to their pursuit of mood enhancers.

As a final footnote to this drug abuse chapter, here's a grim reminder to drug users and Good Samaritan bystanders. Too many of us have learned unconsciously from the implications of pharma's constant messages that there's a pill solution for any problem, and if one pill helps reduce psychological trouble, two pills may even be better. These are marketing persuasions. So listen carefully to the federally required warning within the drug sales pitches. Also ask your pharmacist or primary care physician about any prescription drugs you take.

PART III

Mental Disorders

For the lay person, the mental disorders in this section include a wide range of distortions in thinking and perceiving, mood swings, and marked shifts in activity levels. These observations are easily viewed as strange, peculiar, or weird by the average bystander. A high violence potential or suicide episodes are possible with such symptoms.

These strangers might also seem simply a bit loud and peculiar, yet with normal, seemingly rational speech that warrants a curious glance as you walk by. If observed carefully, the average onlooker wouldn't need professional training to notice a possible, irrational departure from reality suggesting suspicious, paranoia, or possibly grandiose delusions. These borderline symptoms underscore the importance of a 911 call when not sure what to do.

CHAPTER 8

Post-Traumatic Stress Disorder (PTSD)

PTSD has sadly become a popular psychological diagnosis since our occupations of Iraq and Afghanistan. This diagnosis preempts the WWI and II, Korea and Viet Nam shell shock, battle fatigue and other terms used for prolonged combat psychological trauma. PTSD is now also prominently associated with earlier responses to virtually any personally perceived traumatic stress that initially triggers anxiety, shock, terror, guilt, rage, or fear.

The subsequent symptoms of PTSD usually appear in roughly three months or even years later. The duration and severity of symptoms are variable, with observable symptoms lasting for six months or more.

Obsessional ruminations related to the earlier traumatic experience are a major symptom, with residual defensive avoidance of people and situations remotely related to the event. Irritability, insomnia, anger outbursts, startle reactions, and physical symptoms of rapid heart rate, tension, and nausea are noteworthy. Combat PTSD, has also exponentially increased veteran suicides and violent behavior.

Why the startling increase in combat prompted PTSD symptoms in an invasion/occupation situation rather than our more traditional wars, remains debatable. In my professional opinion, however, I believe the differences between previous wars and the more current invasions and occupations are sufficiently significant that it affects U.S. soldiers in markedly different ways. There may be more guilt-laden concerns and anger associated with occupying a country that dangerously resents U.S. presence.

Certainly one personal scenario not particularly difficult to imagine is the soldiers who suffer from a less conventional syndrome of PTSD, not the stereotypically combat-driven. These are the ones who know there's no effective defense against those willing to commit suicide in order to harm you, while occupying their nation that understandably resents your presence. These are the soldiers who probably worry about unseen IED's that can easily and unheroically blow you and your buddies apart, without any fair combat exchange. Then there are the more sinister, nagging, guilt-laden obsessions by our military who have doubts about our unwillingness to leave the occupied countries.

Such doubts, concerns, fears of the unknown, and vague feelings of guilt are sadly understandable, at least to me, as I no longer ponder why so many have succumbed to severe psychological torment and suicide thinking. Consequently, the PTSD syndrome of Iraq and Afghanistan veterans suggest "moral injuries" that are more likely, as documented, to result in suicide and anger-generated violence.

Should you encounter any of the above symptoms in a stranger within the approximate age of our Middle Eastern veterans, keep observing at a distance, and once you call 911, it could be worthwhile to ask if the person is a veteran. Such a question might be viewed as an empathic concern from a sympathetic bystander. Like most syndromes, however, their intensity will vary depending on the person and nature of the traumatic episodes. So observe carefully any stranger's response to your concerns before approaching.

It's also noteworthy that psychological shock symptoms, covered in Chapter 6, are frequently precursors of eventual PTSD if not treated with psychotherapy. Such psychological shock symptoms may also indicate that the stranger you encountered is very vulnerable, while a nearby car accident, injury to someone, or a physical disaster could have also triggered these shock symptoms as listed in Chapter 6.

Your initial observations will no doubt hasten your decision to approach this person, offer help, and tell him/her you have called 911 and will stay until professional assistance arrives. You don't have to be a professional to provide psychological shock victims with such caring reassurance; and in the absence of physical injuries, you don't have to be a qualified first aider to help them stay warm, help them lie down, and elevate their legs a few feet, while awaiting the professionals. If the victim wants to talk to you, simply be a caring listener with gentle reassurances that help is on the way.

As a footnote, you might have imagined as I have, how some of the more anticipated IED injuries may be more terrifying than death. These are the injuries that destroy large intestines or genitals. How emasculating it must be for our young soldiers to return home unable to sexually satisfy their wife or loved one while periodically undergoing medical treatments for the rest of their lives.

CHAPTER 9

Schizophrenia

Schizophrenia is the quintessential "psychotic" mental disorder that's been classified for centuries as *crazies, witches, wackos, loony-tunes,* even *nuts* and more legalistically *insane.* As medical science progressed in sophistication, schizophrenia became a major diagnosis of those descriptions of weird psychotic behaviors.

The disorder has probably endured every possible "intervention" including punishment, confinement as evil through a variety of individual talking therapies. Schizophrenia has become more medicalized in recent years with chemical treatments including Thorazine. Unfortunately, many psychotropic drugs create extra pyramidal side effects, e.g. Tardive Dyskinesia, causing involuntary jerking and spastic movements and gestures; which have resulted in many patients avoiding anti-psychotic drugs. To the average bystander these heavily medicated schizophrenics may look funny or weird as they twitch and jerk their way down the street.

Even today, in the 21st century, medications are the main treatment by the medical establishment. Such drugs seem to have more "management" benefits than actual cures. There also remain the probable side-effects of psychotropic drugs, and whatever the treatment regimen by medicine, group or individual talking therapies along with medications seem to be most successful in reducing symptoms.

Should you, as a bystander, encounter a schizophrenic displaying "crazy" behavior, the person is probably off medications, while revealing some of those twitchy, jerky movements symptomatic of medication side effects. Otherwise, some psychotics may seem zombie-like; which might suggest there's no need for a 911 call. Call anyway if you have any doubts about the stranger's condition or need for an evaluation.

The most typical behaviors of schizophrenia, however, would include possible delusions (thought distortions), hallucinations (visual or auditory), incoherence, disorganized speech, catatonic behavior (seeming motionless as if in a trance), and such additional verbal symptoms like "flat affects" or zombie-like verbal expressions.

Although schizophrenics, similar to most psychotics, are capable of violence, the paranoid and catatonic are especially vulnerable when intimidated by some external stimuli such as an incursive bystander. Otherwise they are "usually" amenable to warm, helpful assistance. The International Classification of Diseases (ICD) and the Diagnostic and Statistical Manual IV (DSM-IV) and very recently published DSM V, have other classifications of psychotic disorders. For the observant bystander, however, many of the above schizophrenic symptoms are recognized rather quickly as "crazy" behaviors warranting professional help. So call 911.

CHAPTER 10

Dissociative Disorders

If you meet someone that seems confused and unable to recall such information as their name, address, marital status, location, etc., you may have encountered symptoms of a dissociative disorder with, in this case, amnesia. Such a disorder can also abruptly prompt a Dissociative Fugue. This condition could have been triggered days or weeks earlier resulting in unintended travel away from one's home, work, and familiar friends while unable to recall the past.

Depersonalizing Disorder is also a non-drug induced series of symptoms related to dissociative disorder. In this case, the victim may also have adequate reality contact but experiences feelings of detachment as if an outside observer of one's body or mental processes. Some such victims view the experience as a dream.

The behaviors of those with dissociative disorders are rarely conspicuous enough to arouse bystander concerns. However, should someone ask for your help, don't assume it's a street hustle, unless he refuses anything but money. Otherwise, simply observe, listen carefully, and call 911.

Although violent behavior is unlikely, any mental disorder with confusion, lack of confidence, disorientation, or memory loss should be approached in a gentle, caring way, while speaking clearly, softly, and slowly.

PART IV

Dementias

These mental conditions are no more dangerous to bystanders than any normal person's remote violent possibilities. The basic mental deficits are a reduced level of intellectual functioning; which may include faulty reasoning with flawed judgments, short and long term memory deficits, attention and concentration problems, etc. Some have such drastically reduced functioning on their own that they need varying degrees of supervision and guidance. They are typically passive, and often childlike.

CHAPTER 11

Mental Retardation

This behavioral deficit is included primarily for your vigilance in helping a person who appears confused, lost, or simply upset, possibly as a result of reduced levels of intellectual functioning. Some may appear child-like while others may seem fearful of any interpersonal contact, generally because of their intellectual difficulties in clearly relating to others. Many have sheltered lives in group homes where they receive appropriate guidance, depending on their psychosocial skill and their responsiveness to training. For some, they live at home where they are cared for with objectives ranging from improved personal hygiene and academic skills, to guidance and training in work programs.

It's also noteworthy that many of the dementias, like mental retardation or Alzheimers may be related to or exacerbated by other medical conditions. In fact, all of these conditions, under stress, can result in similar symptoms of disorientation, feeling overwhelmed, and in desperate need of sympathetic guidance. These mentally handicapped subjects may present as a "lost child," and a 911 call, with gentle support and guidance, is typically advisable.

CHAPTER 12

Alzheimer's Type

This condition has become increasingly popularized in recent years; and it is included in this book to clarify some of the layperson's misunderstandings associated with some of its symptoms.

Many of my "old" friends seem to have a touch of "hypocondriacal" alzheimers. This is suggested by their chronic concerns that standing quizzically in front of their open refrigerator may be the first symptom of the dreaded disease—Alzheimers. Well readers and future Good Samaritans, I believe worrying about such symptoms is counter-productive. It's like worrying about going blind because you need reading glasses. As we age, our brain and body begin to gradually deteriorate, and although we all mentally decline at different paces, if we live long enough, we'll probably experience some symptoms of Mild Cognitive Impairment (MCI,) like staring vaguely at an open refrigerator, forgetting your keys, coat, or other articles, etc., or unable to recall the names of people you've recently met. Alzheimers, on the other hand, may, for the bystander, be described as the pathological extreme of some cognitive deterioration we all worry about as we age.

Properly diagnosed symptoms of Alzheimers will include seriously impaired memory with an inability to learn unfamiliar information. Those inflicted may also exhibit such cognitive dysfunctions as Aphasia (language problems), Apraxia (impaired motor activity even though motor functioning is not impaired), Agnosia (cannot recognize familiar objects despite intact sensory functions), and poor executive functioning (includes inability to organize, plan, and understand stimulus inputs).

The decline in many of these behaviors keeps deteriorating relentlessly; which ultimately impairs social and occupational functioning. There's also a psychological concept that further tends to separate Alzheimers victims from those with Mild Cognitive Impairment. The psychological symptom is called Confabulations, which means: subjects tend to fill in gaps in their memory with possible delusional ideas. Such confabulations are indicative of mild impairments that can become a serious behavioral disturbance, since such subjects may tend to eventually believe their confabulations.

It's also noteworthy that bystanders who observe someone with Alzheimers or dementia wandering about as if lost, they probably are. You certainly need to make a 911 call, along with reassuring comments to the confused person, e.g. "I'll stay with you and help you in any way I can until professional help arrives," etc.

As a footnote to readers of this section, the probability of having the most debilitating of alzheimers symptoms by age 65 is 1 in 9; which are comforting odds against being an alzheimers invalid, provided you keep exercising your mind and body.

PART V

Second Aid for those you know

Similar to Psychological First Aid, second aid begins with our observations, that vital assessment strategy is fundamental to the accuracy of any behavioral interventions. Of course, different from observations of a stranger, before and after comparisons are essential in second aid.

Acknowledging a troubled friend's need for help may depend on recognizing subtle behavioral changes not usually apparent to a casual acquaintance.

CHAPTER 13

Assessment and Intervention

Unless we're some sort of hermit, we all tend to have some friends, loved ones, relatives, or coworkers that somehow impact our lives; and each of these familiar individuals has a definable personality, regardless of their age. They may be shy or outgoing, typically negative or positive, interesting or boring, well-groomed or unkempt, animated, slow, talkative, or reticent. They might even be characterized more reflectively as happy-go-lucky, or melancholy, humorous, somber, cranky, shallow, aprosodic (zombie-like speech without melody), profound, or charismatic.

These are all personality characteristics that pretty much define each of us by a wide variety of observable behaviors. Just observing these behaviors over time offers "base line" descriptions of their typical personality, including verbal and nonverbal mannerisms. Then, should behavioral changes occur, your previous observations could reveal those subtle or gross, before and after behavioral differences.

For example, based on your observations, a good friend since college has consistently been considered an exceptionally outgoing, good-humored, clean-shaven, well-read guy in his sixties. He has, however, become noticeably quiet, with delayed humorless replies to jokes, and a loss of interest in world affairs. Should his behavioral changes be mentioned by you, his friend? Absolutely!

He may be despondent over another friend or relative. He may have discovered a serious medical issue, financial concerns, etc. It doesn't really matter. For now, since he hasn't confided in you, your first move is to simply let him know that you're aware of his possible behavioral differences, that you may be over-reacting, yet if something is really wrong, you are willing to assist him in any way. He should also know that you're just a dear friend who doesn't intend to intrude into his life unless needed. Such comments gently acknowledge your concern, while offering to help, along with a respect for the friend's privacy. Such an unintrusive, concerned approach may invite the dialogue you are seeking. If not, a simplistic, sincere assurance that you are always there if needed, may be supportive enough until your friend is ready.

Here's another second aid example that may be more delicate, with possible unintended consequences: Living in a house where there's a child, you might begin to notice what you consider prominent changes in behavior. Assessment of changes in children's behavior, however, is a bit tricky since behavioral strategies and personalities, like their physical appearance, are continuing to develop. A child's behavior and physical appearance can also be more fragile and less stable than adult behaviors. Again, continued observations may verify your suspicions.

Noteworthy physical changes in weight, eating habits, or repeated ailments, withdrawal, mood swings, etc. should initially be pursued with concerned unchallenging feedback to parents and gentle inquiries regarding current or future medical appointments. Discussions with the child's friends and other relatives may also be advisable depending on parental responsiveness.

The diagnostic possibilities may seem endless, including neighborhood or school bullies, a family friend or relative sexual predator, dietary problems, even abusive parents, etc. However, it's not advisable for you, as a Good Samaritan, to probe for underlying causes by interrogating the child. The best you can do initially is to keep observing the child with frequent chats, assurances you're an adult friend that just wants to help the child stay happy, etc.

Also while observing the child's behavior and relationships with others, an accurate recording of the child's continued symptoms could eventually be worthwhile, and should the behavior noticeably deteriorate, it may be time again to more urgently discuss your concerns and observations with relatives.

If parents and other relatives are indifferent to or in denial of "obvious" symptoms of some sort of pathological changes, the next step may be critical to both the child and your relationship with the relatives. It now warrants what I described earlier as the 3 C's for any Good Samaritan. Remember? They stand for common sense, compassion, and courage.

If you genuinely believe the child's now obvious symptoms are being ignored by significant others, your options are the following: If the child is in school or day care with responsible professionals, inquire about any behavioral changes in the child and present your personal concerns and quandary. If the school authorities refuse to discuss the child since you're not a relative, insist that they at least call the parents or observe the child more closely. Should you have the courage to pursue your concerns further; common sense will no doubt warn you that your relationship with the entire family may collapse, especially if you're wrong. If, however, you sincerely believe the child is in some kind of physical or psychological danger, it's time to call the local Child Protective Agency.

If school or day care professionals have still failed to contact parents, while you continue to have some unresolved doubts, simply keep closely observing and chatting with the child who may finally acknowledge his/her problem. As your last resort call 911, unless you actually witness child abuse. Then don't hesitate to immediately call 911!

Footnote reminders:

1. Observation of those we know remains critical information in comparing before and after behaviors.

2. Any kind of observed behavioral changes, especially if abrupt, may suggest an underlying disturbance.
3. Initially, simply comment on your observed behavioral changes.
4. If no acknowledgement, don't probe, just keep observing.
5. Should behaviors seem to worsen, be gentle and sincere with such comments as "I need your   friendship…If something's troubling you, I'm always here to help."
6. In observing children, be patient; casually inquire to parents, etc. in a nonthreatening way, with a call to Child Protection Agency if reasonably sure the child needs help and parents openly resist.
7. 911 may be your last resort, provided you either witness abuse or the child finally confides in you.

CHAPTER 14

Suicide Prevention

As a final solution to life's problems, suicide deserves a separate chapter in this Second Aid section. Third Millennium research indicates that despite advances in treatment of depression, suicides in the U.S. remain a complex multifaceted mental disorder that too frequently fails to be diagnosed until the victim's ultimate solution is final. This underscores an indispensible mantra in suicide prevention: If you know anyone who has even hinted suicidal thoughts, listen carefully, then listen again. Always take such comments very seriously, be supportive, and assist your friend, relative, or neighbor to find alternative solutions through professional organizations or a therapist. If their behavior or replies suggest suicide is imminent, call 911 immediately *and stay with the person* until professional help arrives. Ironically, other than the above high risk suicidal symptoms, a behavioral change to a more self-reliant, comfortable demeanor may signal impending suicide. It's not unusual for a distraught victim to feel relieved once he completes a definite suicide plan.

High suicide potential, however, is usually preceded by more subtle, less obvious suicidal risk behaviors that are only recognized by those who are acquainted with the person's overall, more typical behaviors. Consequently, reviewing the below psychologically researched list of suicidal risk clues is provided before discussing actual prevention interventions.

- Men are a higher suicide risk than women.
- Teenagers, into their mid-twenties, and seniors over sixty-five are more prone to suicide than other ages.
- Intoxication: Many suicides are associated with alcohol as a contributing factor; an even greater number may be associated with the presence of alcohol without the actual mention of suicide.
- Special clinical populations: Someone who has been sexually involved with a prior therapist, those with AIDS, and more recently, returning military from the Iraqi and Afghan "wars" may also have an increased risk of suicide.
- In the United States, whites tend to have the highest suicide rates, while Native American suicide is "greater than other ethnic groups in the U.S. especially in the age range of 15 to 24 years."
- Suicide risk clearly increases when someone is living alone, and is reduced significantly if a mother has children living with her.
- Bereavement clearly increases suicide risk, and suicide rates are lower for the grieving wife than for a husband who has lost his spouse, especially among elderly men.
- Unemployment, as well as illnesses and somatic complaints, increase the risk of suicide.
- Other stressful events, such as sexual assault, have resulted in attempted suicides by the female victim.
- There is a high risk of suicide when a patient is released from hospitalization for a weekend family visit or discharge.

Having read the above high suicide risk indicators, you probably feel much better informed yet even more concerned about preventing or at least reducing the probability of suicide. Unfortunately, like most aberrant behaviors, there aren't any cookbook strategies to prevent suicidal attempts even when the symptoms are clear.

There's no doubt one axiom you've learned from this book, that there's no clear cut guaranteed remedy to any mental or physical distress, other than the one final solution you're trying to prevent. And that's the ultimate conundrum!

For some people it may be too late for an effective intervention. The victim has tried to remove the intense psychological or physical pain for years and nothing seems to work. There are also the victims who, in a fit of despair, rage, or impulse, kill themselves before trying alternatives. My point is that all individuals who seem suicidal deserve help, while realizing that even professional treatment may not be successful for a variety of reasons, including the person just needs to die.

Even though this chapter on suicide prevention may be focused on those you know, it's really everyone's responsibility to somehow help reduce suicides, homicides, senseless Aurora, Columbine, Tucson, and Newtown, Connecticut mass carnage, drunken driving massacres, sexual predators, etc. in their early stages of symptom development.

As suggested in earlier chapters, such interventions actually begin long before symptoms are apparent during those formative years, when the entire community has shared responsibility for the welfare of each other. The potential for violently dangerous, mentally chaotic behaviors may begin with the birth of an unwanted child, vulnerable to parental abuse. Moreover, there's a high probability that stable, nurturing parents with close, positive interactions with their children greatly reduce later mental health related violence potential to themselves or others.

Genetics, however, may also contribute to increased severe behavior problems later in life when too many neighbors, friends, and bystanders failed to acknowledge symptom peculiarities with even a 911 call.

Research further suggests that neighbors who tend to care for each other have significantly less mental health problems and domestic violence. In my professional experiences throughout the world, I've been consistently delighted in any neighborhood by the wonders of a smile, a wave, or a friendly willingness to help someone who seemed lost or troubled.

It's painfully obvious that compassionate, readily accessible neighbors in most communities can markedly contribute to a reduction in high violence potential, including suicides. However, once someone you know begins exhibiting symptoms, a suicide prevention strategy becomes urgent and may depend more on your relationship with the potential victim than verbal suggestions and support.

Most important to remember, however, is if their behavior or replies suggest a suicide attempt is imminent, call 911 and stay with the person until professional help arrives. Otherwise, as stated earlier, always take any suicide hints seriously, and try to persuade him or her to obtain professional help, while offering realistic support and loyalty as you interact as a friend, not a therapist. Professionals are well aware that psychotherapy isn't a pure science, and should your friend commit suicide following your sincere advice or comments, you just may suffer the ordeal of blaming yourself. Yes, some suicidal friends will resolutely kill themselves regardless of treatment intervention; and although professionals also grieve, they're better prepared than a friend if a patient's need to die is finalized.

CHAPTER 15

High Violence Potential

Eminent

Unarguably, one of the major concerns of any potential psychological first aider is the possibility of being harmed while trying to help a weird-acting stranger. Such a caution is both understandable and an essential part of Chapter 5's Mental Status Examination (MSE). Determining the vulnerability of a victim as well as the safety of others are the two vital reasons for carefully observing the bizarrely behaving stranger, and why calling 911 is essential if either possibility might exist.

Since you learned in Chapter 5 that searching for symptoms by observation is the first thing you do when you encounter a possible victim, it's also your most important initial activity before moving any closer to the stranger. Your MSE in Chapter 5 suggested you're searching for any behaviors and physical characteristics that may give you a behavioral portrait. You will also be scanning for cues (symptoms) that might be related to a specific syndrome. For our potential Good Samaritan bystander, symptoms related to high violence danger always have the highest priority when deciding how physically close to go in helping a stranger.

So, regardless of other diagnostic considerations, the following observable behavioral cues may have the most significant indications of eminent high violence.

- Any signs of visible tension, e.g. clinched fists, gnashing teeth, or grinding jaws, wide-eyed, wild starring, other signs of muscular tension, pacing or strutting, shouting, loud talking or mumbling, or swearing. Other troublesome precursors of possible aggression include grasping any object, e.g. stick, rock, other weapons, etc, disheveled appearance, messed hair, torn clothes, blood splatter, bare feet, etc.
- Other less obvious signs of tension may be noteworthy indicators of violence potential; however, any stranger exhibiting a limp, loose, sluggish demeanor, and a clear response to questions, suggests a probable absence of high violence potential.
- Incoherent ramblings, repetitive gestures or movements, glances or stares that don't seem directed at anyone, mumblings as if to some nonexistent object, etc. may suggest unpredictable psychotic behavior. Such observed behavior may suggest to the professional delusional thinking, hallucinations, even homicidal or suicidal thinking.
- It is also noteworthy that sitting virtually motionless on the street or sidewalk while seemingly unresponsive to others may unpredictably erupt into violent behavior.

A few minutes of observation should elicit enough of the above symptoms to then quickly call 911 while maintaining a safe distance! Here's an important reminder and caveat. When in doubt about a stranger suddenly becoming violent, always err on the side of your safety and become a Good Samaritan by maintaining a safe distance and calling 911. Common sense and professional literature should also remind you, there are no observable symptom patterns that can guarantee an accurate prediction of violent or nonviolent behavior. The predictive validity of future behavior from present behavior isn't an exacting science, however like most science, outcomes are based on probabilities which, in life decisions, sure beats tossing a coin.

Future

For readers who aren't convinced that it's important to report even mild displays of peculiar behavior of strangers, the remainder of this chapter on the "shaping of violent behavior" that may occur in the future should be of special interest.

Recent mass killings of innocent strangers have finally aroused our entire nation with marked uneasiness, wariness, and deep sympathy for those in endless grieving. A prevention or intervention strategy for the mentally disturbed during their mass murders is obviously years too late. These psychologically troubled assassins were probably vulnerable to explosive killings from birth, because of some unknown genetic predisposition that fortunately seems to affect relatively few. Their violence potential may remain dormant unless awakened by a dysfunctional environment—loaded with triggers. Then, such a vulnerable person may begin to gradually develop pathological symptoms to cope with external stressors. These signs of mental problems can occur during early youth, and, without treatment, symptoms will likely become increasingly serious, eventually erupting into mass violence and as often, suicide.

Our gender is biologically defined by our genes, and virtually all of these U.S. mass killers have been male. As infants they were cuddly, fragile, and vulnerable to those countless external influences that may eventually contribute to their final deadly, mental disorders, and adult high violence behavior.

As suggested above, preventing random killings of individuals remains regretfully unlikely, yet reducing the intensity, magnitude, and frequency of such carnage is certainly tenable. We do know, with a high degree of certainty, that although the predictive validity of mass killings isn't too promising at this time, we must profit by our mistakes and keep trying.

As bystanders, most people will encounter a strange-behaving person occasionally in their life; and different from helping the physically injured, too often a bystander's dismissive response is "it's none of my business." This may be another reason many troubled persons, shunned or avoided by others, rarely receive comprehensive treatment, while feeling uneasy around people, including professionals.

Identifying some of the early common behavioral patterns of mass killers could be indispensible in eventually creating a high violence potential profile. Obviously a few of such behaviors may apply to most of us, but as the number of symptoms increase, so does the possibility of subsequent violent behavior.

Although the following represents some of the known characteristics of mass murderers with the highest predicted validity, such a list is neither scientifically complete nor based solely on rigorous research. As in all mental health science, however, researchers have to start somewhere:

- Male gender.
- At least above average intelligence.
- Cruelty to animals.
- School problems relating to peers or staff.
- Bullied by other students.
- No close friends.
- Occasional incoherent ramblings at home or in public.
- No known girlfriends.
- Depressive episodes with feelings of alienation by peers.
- Interest in fire arms.
- Delusional paranoid—ramblings.
- Scholastically well above average.
- No school sports activities.
- Suicide ideations.

In summary, every bystander, friend, or relative can observe strange, weird, or bizarre behavior without any professional training. Consequently, it is "all of our business" to immediately call 911 should you feel suspicious or just uneasy in realizing that a person's strange behaviors may some day erupt into catastrophic killings.

Records further indicate these mass killers "rarely" received significant mental treatment. It's also noteworthy that parents, school peers, even neighbors all influence any child's development and behavioral changes.

PART VI
The Mental Health Paradox

If we, as a nation, carefully considered all of the economic and therapeutic costs associated with mental illness, the actual bill just might eclipse the medical health costs in our country. Then again, probably not, and here are some of the more obvious reasons.

As hinted throughout this book, the overwhelming majority of us have an abundance of sympathy for people with physical illness or injuries. If we see some guy hesitatingly trying to tap his way across the street with his white cane, virtually all those nearby would experience a tinge of pity and a readiness to guide the stranger across the street and beyond. If, on the other hand, an obvious drunk or weird-behaving guy was attempting to cross the same heavily trafficked street, few if any bystanders would help, except perhaps one of those Good Samaritans. Sadly, we tend to remain sympathetic to those with physical problems, while ignoring weird behavioral expressions of mental disorders.

The bottom line seems to be that people with physical injuries or diseases either recognize their problems and seek help or, as soon as others recognize the physical symptoms, such a victim is immediately taken to an emergency room or urgent care for initial diagnosis and treatment. The mentally ill, however, with resultant behavioral problems, RARELY refer themselves for treatment, while too many bystanders and friends are just as hesitant to even suggest they find mental assistance.

CHAPTER 16

Mental Health is all of our Business

I certainly agree that weird behaving strangers can seem scary, if not annoying, yet for their own safety, as well as the safety of others, mentally, emotionally, and weird behaving strangers need professional evaluations as an initial treatment step. Otherwise, if interventions are ignored, such behaviors are likely to worsen, similar to an untreated infection or a potential mass killer.

As I mentioned in an earlier chapter, there have been numerous documented accounts of no one even calling the police as a screaming women in a populated neighborhood was being sexually assaulted. Professional mental health training of law enforcement has also been lacking, as evidenced by police who have shot and killed strange behaving, mentally troubled individuals who weren't brandishing a dangerous weapon. Thankfully, many law enforcement agencies throughout our nation are finally receiving training in recognizing the mentally disturbed and how to protect them from harming others.

It's also well known that many school kids have demonstrated the amazing value of Red Cross First Aid books in helping the sick and injured, yet learning invaluable information for these youngsters about the perils of seduction by child molesters who are typically family friends or relatives, continues to remain inadequate. The Sandusky, Penn State sexual molestations and their cover-ups aren't unusual. They were simply more publicized and outrageous.

Then there are drunk drivers, domestic violence, animal abuses, the marginally functioning, otherwise unremarkable ordinary citizens of every age, race, and both genders. Those are the mentally troubled individuals we've all known or noticed throughout our lives. Early in their development, symptoms may have been mild with progressively more serious symptoms if their disturbances remain untreated. They are stumbling along as best they can, moderately confused and sometimes overwhelmed with worry about their coping abilities, while unable to understand or find help for those deep feelings of alienation. They are usually lower middle class, hard workers, without any significant arrests. Can their earlier symptoms later erupt into unimaginable mass killings of innocents? I'm afraid so.

Often such victims of our society's external pressures and social demands turn to their primary care physician for help. Unfortunately the help they generally receive is a prescription for some sort of medication like an antidepressant. This treatment approach may be understandable for the primary care physician with a heavy case load and routine 5 to 10 minute sessions with patients. These physicians, however, were not trained in medical school to treat mental health problems. Worse yet, even when prescribed by a qualified mental health professional, such drugs are not particularly effective in actually treating underlying reasons for the mental illness, while sending a pervasively flawed message in our society that pills solve every day behavioral problems. In fact, many illegal drug dealers are pushing prescription drugs as a more profitable business, while TV medication commercials are no doubt contributing to the increasing competition between illegal and legal drugs.

If physicians prefer to keep their referrals in the medical family, board qualified psychiatrists are certainly more appropriate in prescribing and carefully monitoring any drugs administered. There are also social workers, mental health counselors, psychologists, and other mental health professionals well-qualified to diagnose and engage in psychotherapy. Research demonstrates that psychotherapy is very effective in helping the moderately troubled patient without drugs and their possible dangerous side effects.

Ψ Ψ Ψ

The preceding represents some examples of the enormous number and variety of mental health problems affecting all ages in our increasingly complex, stress-provoking society. When one considers the residual costs of incarceration, locked mental health facilities, court procedures, the high violence potential of troubled students and psychotic adults, as well as the endless and costly war on drugs, it seems as if we still haven't recognized that our mental health problems are astronomically expensive in lives and money. Hopefully, the evidence clearly indicates that, if all of us ordinary citizens simply acknowledge a mental health crisis in our country, it would be a good start in fixing the problem.

Moreover, I earnestly believe it's "all of our business and responsibility" to help prevent the Jared Loughner random killings and maiming of innocents in Tucson; the murder of fellow service personnel by Major Nidal M. Hasan, a psychiatrist at Fort Hood Texas; James Holmes' equally senseless carnage against strangers during a Batman midnight movie; and the horrific murder of 20 children and 6 adults at the Sandy Hook Elementary School by a troubled 20-year-old, Adam Lanza. These senseless slaughters underscored another serious national concern with their many mental health implications.

These assassins weren't international terrorists, Taliban, or al Qaida enemies, etc. They were all psychologically severely disturbed, clearly delusional young men whose distortion of reality deteriorated into catastrophic carnage. Long before the explosive massacres by these four men, they had undoubtedly displayed symptom peculiarities recognized by friends, relatives, coworkers and even bystanders. Yet no noteworthy evaluations or treatment interventions apparently occurred.

Could early warnings by others, including bystanders, have prevented or reduced such senseless slaughter? Although health professionals obviously can't offer any certainties, early detection, reporting of abnormal behaviors and resultant treatment could have made a definite preventive difference! As suggested throughout this book, each of us ordinary, law-abiding citizens can help delay treatment for the mentally ill with our dismissive silence. On the other hand, we can help the mentally disturbed obtain early treatment by making mental health and mass killings "all of our business."

I doubt if any of you remember one of the earlier mass murders, it's sadly worth reviewing. It occurred in 1966 at the University of Texas by an engineering student who murdered his wife and mother before shooting at anyone from the university clock tower. There he managed to kill 14 more innocents and wound 32. The unforgettable irony of his rampage, however, is in the content of his suicide note that 47 years later still resonates a vital message to anyone concerned about preventing potential mass killings:

"I have been a victim of many unusual and irrational thoughts...and if my life insurance policy is valid please pay off my debts...donate the rest anonymously to a mental health foundation. Maybe research can prevent further tragedies of this type."

An appropriate summary of this chapter is a recent, well-researched article by Ed Vega, Executive Director of the Mental Health Association of San Francisco. Here are some of the main points.

- Mental illness affects nearly every family in the United States.
- One in four people will have a serious mental health condition that could be improved with treatment; however, less than 30% of these seek help.

- There is a definite interaction between mental, emotional, and physical health.

Finally, the following is representative of the mental health dilemma in our country. On a 2012 warm, peaceful autumn day in Bullhead City, Arizona, a beautiful Blue Heron was sipping water from a golf course pond, when a fairly unremarkable-looking man started to walk by the bird, then stopped. He literally bludgeoned the Blue Heron to death with one of his golf clubs.

Some Good Samaritan bystanders called security and the guy eventually went to court. He was fined $450, with no incarceration for even one day, no probation supervision, or any type of treatment evaluation or intervention—just a fine that someone might receive for an ordinary moving traffic violation.

Apparently it wasn't sufficiently news worthy to be reported in national newspapers. We can all agree that this guy has a high violence potential as evidenced by sadistically bizarre behavior symptoms treated with just a $450 fine. Without clinical treatment, could he become another mass killer? Since prior behavior represents a high probability of similar future behavior, I hesitate to say no. Next case!

EPILOGUE

A not too subtle message throughout this book has been our responsibility to help others in desperate need the best we can! This human imperative applies to virtually all of us of any age, race, or gender.

Hopefully you have also learned that, starting with your family and neighborhood, we are all bystanders with Good Samaritan potential to protect others. Moreover, what you have acquired in previous chapters about both your limitations and increased familiarity with the behavioral problems of others expands your Good Samaritan readiness to any community, not just your neighborhood.

Just so you won't lose your willingness to help others, the following will provide you with a summary of those indispensible core ideas contained in each of the previous chapters.

Major Reminders
- We are all potential Good Samaritans provided we give assistance within the limits of our own mental and physical abilities.
- Trying to help a physically or mentally injured person beyond your skill level often does more harm than good.
- Since some mentally troubled strangers may have obvious physical injuries, a basic American Red Cross First Aid book or course will enrich your confidence and ability to help others.

- Careful observation of mentally or physically troubled behavior is the most vital diagnostic tool before making those assist or desist decisions.
- Affective second aid requires awareness by careful observation of both before and after behaviors.
- Crazy (psychotic) looking behaviors may suggest a high violence potential, so before distancing yourself, at least call 911.
- In second aid any obvious behavioral changes in a friend or relative, especially if abrupt, may suggest an underlying mental or physical disturbance.
- Should you witness abuse of a child or anyone's plea for help, take them seriously and call 911 immediately.
- Ignoring the drunks, bums, and weirdoes as "none of my business" exacerbates our country's mental health crisis.
- Animal cruelty is a serious signal of eventual high violence potential against humans.
- Don't forget that strange acting youth could be a symptom of a subsequent mass killer without treatment.
- Help reduce mental health problems and potential mass killings by never hesitating to call 911 when noticing weird, suspicious, or potentially violent behavior.
- Virtually all of those who committed the well-known random massacres of innocent victims exhibited earlier mental symptoms that remained untreated.
- Finally, having read this book entitles you to Good Samaritan status.

CONGRATULATIONS!

ADDENDUM

These additional comments to the Epilogue are some further reminders of the relentless massacres of strangers and the endless need to transform all bystanders into Good Samaritans.

While in the process of revising a few pages before formatting and final publication, I heard of some other senseless killing and maiming. During the Boston Marathon in April 2013 the carnage was 200 innocents. Since then I've learned that there were two brothers of Chechen heritage allegedly responsible for the bombings. They apparently used homemade bombs, then a gun to kill an MIT campus police officer.

Although the devastation has terrorist, Islamic implications against the U.S., the formal investigation continues, with more critical similarities than differences to other U.S. mass killings, including the Oklahoma bombing by Timothy McVey.

In comparing mass killers, one similarity is that the underlying reasons for all the recent carnage, including the Boston Marathon massacre, may never be clearly understood. Also, the killings were caused by individuals who apparently were not associated with actual terrorist organizations, and both firearms and homemade bombs were involved.

These essential similarities once again indicate that mass killings, regardless of the underlying reasons or magnitude of the carnage, cannot be totally prevented no matter how many National Guard, police, fire fighters, or FBI agents patrol the streets.

Then in May and June, 2013 two separate deaths by gunfire clearly underscore the other obvious contributors to random, inexplicable killings—because of guns' seductively easy access and use by children. In May, a five-year-old child shot and killed his two year old sister, while playing with the 22 caliber single shot rifle he received for his birthday. In June, a four-year-old boy shot and killed his Special Forces veteran father with a gun he found in the home of his dad's friend during a visit. Such killings are certainly not unusual, and since neither child is to blame for the killings, I consider them victims of irresponsible adults with children who viewed such dangerous weapons as harmless toys. In fact, research indicates that hundreds of kids are "accidentally" killed each year in similar manners, while such tragedies are rarely mentioned as easily preventable by parents who are entrusted with the protection of their offspring.

I personally underscore these two killings because of their paradoxical prelude to many mass killings. It's simply too easy to kill someone with a gun. Virtually any four-year-old has the finger strength to pull a gun's trigger. Even killing a father with a gun is that simple—too simple. Guns are just plain too accessible, invitingly easy to fire, and excessively promoted, even encouraged, as one of our "constitutional rights."

If you've read all of these tragedies before, consider my comments, like commercials, reminders of the extreme danger of guns in irresponsible, criminal, mentally disturbed, or children's tiny hands.

Maybe it's time to keep repeating these tragedies until ordinary, concerned citizens are acknowledged by the majority of our representatives.

Finally, it's unlikely that the most alert, capable professional street patrols and surveillance equipment can possibly match the vigilance available by crowds of concerned ordinary bystanders on city streets or in well-publicized, congested sports activities. If just aware that their wandering observations are vital to the security of themselves and others, these bystanders become the *first actual observers* against high violence potential behaviors. Bystanders in any crowded city typically precede all those professionally trained EMT's, police, fire fighters, and trained volunteers—those *first responders.*

Having just said all that in this addendum has provided me with an indispensible conclusion:

In any community, bystanders are indispensible for the safety and sense of security they offer by their sheer watchful presence as possible Good Samaritans; and all that's required is come observation skills, a concern for others, and a readiness to dial 911.

THE END

GLOSSARY

Here are a few terms that you'll read so often in this book; it seemed worthwhile to define them early on.

First Aid is traditionally viewed as the initial assistance given to anyone, generally administered by a stranger probably with no professional preparation, to a stranger whose potentially serious injury or ailment has received no previous professional assistance. First aid usually occurs after a victim is injured, in physical distress, exhibiting symptoms such as unconsciousness or bleeding.

Psychological First Aid is a more recent term when the "first responder" i.e. the first person to help a victim, encounters a victim exhibiting bizarre behaviors that may require a calming strategy.

The general term first aid may include administering CPR, controlling bleeding, calming an emotionally traumatized person, calling 911, asking other bystanders to assist, or any stabilizing procedure while awaiting a professional emergency vehicle.

Second Aid: Assisting, friends, acquaintances, family members, with preexisting injuries, ailments or behavior problems. Also, follow up assistance to some stranger you offered First aid earlier.

CPR: Cardiopulmonary Resuscitation. Refer to American Red Cross Manual.

Heimlich Maneuver: Upper stomach compressions to dislodge object in throat. Refer to American Red Cross manual for details.

REFERENCES

The books and manuals below may help you expand your psychological first aid knowledge and interest, including assistance in disasters by disaster response workers, and updated first aid books.

1. *Psychological First Aid Field Operations Guide*, Second Edition, July, 2006. www.natsn.org. and www.neptsd.va.gov

2. *Emergency First Aid Guide, A Family Guide to First Aid and Emergency*, and *Masters of Disaster Educators Kit*. You can order any of the above first aid books at a 20% discount on www.redcross.org.

3. *Diagnostic Criteria from DSM-IV-TR*, (Diagnostic and Statically Manual of Mental Disorders) American Psychiatric Association, 1410 K Street, N.W., Washington, DC 20005.

4. *Human Aggression and Violence, Causes, Manifestations, and Consequences*. Shaver and Mario, MIKULIN. APA (American Psychological Association), 1-800-374-2721. www.apa.org/pubs/books.

5. *Trauma Therapy in Context. The Science and Practice of Evidence-based Practice* (Treating Trauma Survivors) APA, ISBN 978-1-4338-1143-2.

6. *Treatment of Post-Traumatic Stress Disorder in Special Populations*. APA
ISBN 978-1-4338-0464-9.

7. *San Francisco Tenderloin,* Expanded Second Edition, Larry Wonderling, Ph.D.,
ISBN 978-0-9659425-6-3.

8. *The American Red Cross First Aid and Safety Manual,* Brown, Little and Company, New York, Boston, London.

9. *Minding Your Matter,* Dr. Larry Wonderling, Ph.D., ISBN 0-9659415-7-4.

10. *Seductive Illusions,* Dr. Lawrence Wonderling, ISBN 0-9659414-0-7.

11. *Perfect Health-Complete Mind Body Guide,* Deepak Chopra, Three Rivers Press, 2000.

12. *Body for Life, 12 Weeks to Mental and Physical Strength,* Bill Phillips, Harper Collins, 1999.

13. *Natural Health, Natural Medicine—A Comprehensive Manual for wellness and Self-Care,* Andrew Weil, Houghton Mifflin Co. 1995.

14. *Psychological First Aid, How to Care for and Support the Victims of Incidents,* Dr. Eva Roman, Global Management Enterprises LLC, 2005.   Despite the title similarity this book focuses on the training of care givers who have prepared to assist psychologically traumatized victims of disasters, including shocking incidents.

15. *Diagnostic and Statistical Manual of Mental Disorders, Fifth Edition* DSM-5, Copyright © 2013, American Psychiatric Association.

Psychological First Aid
And the Good Samaritan

ABOUT THE AUTHOR

Dr. Wonderling is one of those rare professionals with a variety of different careers and plenty of street savvy. As a mediocre high school student he excelled in athletics with later inductions into high school and college football halls of fame. Still mediocre academically, he managed a BA college degree in Sociology and physical education. Then drafted into the Korean War, he served as a field counselor for traumatized combat soldiers and as a football coach. When discharged, his work with emotionally troubled soldiers guided him away from a sports career to an MS degree in psychology. He was finally academically motivated to help others. In his spare time, however, he enjoyed competitive skiing, ski patrol, ocean sailing, and national race car driving—for over 20 years.

After a decade in the criminal justice system as parole agent, probation officer and psychologist in several maximum security prisons, Dr. Wonderling obtained his PhD in clinical psychology and a private practice with drunks, junkies, and a wide variety of mentally disturbed social rejects in the rough San Francisco Tenderloin.

He also worked as a Peace Corps consultant psychologist for fifteen years, resulting in assignments throughout the world including Afghanistan, Swaziland, Ghana, Morocco, and both central and south America. In addition to assisting troubled volunteers, he gained an international reputation as a cross cultural speaker and a human relations program developer.

He is a critically acclaimed author with seven publications since his retirement, and a columnist for a local Prescott magazine for over five years. At 83, he remains in fine health, with a frequent comment to interviewers: "Don't ever retire, just turn your priority list upside down and follow those long delayed interests!"

If you have any questions at all about the information in this book, please do not hesitate to contact the author, Dr. Wonderling. His email address is:

capfound@aol.com

Publisher

www.ingramcontent.com/pod-product-compliance
Lightning Source LLC
Chambersburg PA
CBHW052045270326
41931CB00012B/2643